Practical Ma

CARTOMANCY

Prediction Through Playing Cards

RK Sharma

Practical Manual of Cartomancy

DEDICATION

To my beloved family,

Thank you for being my inspiration and my rock throughout this entire journey. Your unwavering love and support have been my guiding light, and I could not have accomplished this without you.

You have been with me through the long hours of writing and the moments of doubt and frustration. You have listened to me ramble on about plotlines and characters, and your encouragement has been invaluable.

This book is a tribute to you, and to our love. May it serve as a testament to the depth of our connection and the beauty of our shared experiences. I dedicate this book to you, my Mother, my Inspiration, and my greatest source of joy.

With Love and Light
RK Sharma

CONTENTS

ACKNOWLEDGMENTS

I would like to express my gratitude to the many people who have helped and supported me throughout the creation of this book.
First and foremost, I want to thank my family for their constant love and encouragement. Your belief in me has been unwavering, and I could not have done this without you.

I would also like to thank my friends for their support and encouragement, especially those who provided feedback on early drafts of the manuscript. Your insights and suggestions helped to shape this book into what it is today.

My heartfelt appreciation also goes out to my editor and the entire publishing team for their hard work and dedication. Your guidance and expertise have been invaluable.

Finally, I would like to acknowledge the readers of this book. It is an honor and a privilege to share my work with you, and I hope that it brings you joy, inspiration, and new insights.

Thank you all for being a part of this journey with me.

With Love and Light

RK   Sharma

CHAPTER : 1

INTRODUCTION OF CARTOMANCY

- Meaning of Cartomancy
- What is Cartomancy ?
- Benefits of Cartomancy.
- Scope of Cartomancy.
- Cartomancy Tools

Practical Manual of Cartomancy

What is the meaning of Cartomancy?

The word "Cartomancy" is derived from the French word "Carte" meaning "card" and the Greek word "Manteia" meaning "divination". So, the literal meaning of "Cartomancy" is "divination using cards".

What is Cartomancy ?

Cartomancy is divination technique by which a Reader guides, counsels, Motivates and predicts by the help of instincts, intuition and Playing Cards.

Benefits of Cartomancy ?

Cartomancy is believed to offer several benefits to individuals who practice it or seek guidance from a cartomancer. Some potential benefits of cartomancy include:

Insight and Guidance: Cartomancy can provide insight and guidance on various aspects of life, such as love, career, finances, and relationships. It can help individuals make informed decisions and gain a new perspective on their problems or situations.

Self-Discovery: Cartomancy can aid in self-discovery by uncovering hidden truths, feelings, or aspects of the self. It can help individuals understand their own motivations, strengths, and weaknesses.

Clarity and Focus: Cartomancy can bring clarity and focus to a person's life by helping them identify and prioritize their goals and objectives. It can help individuals develop a clearer understanding of what they want and how to achieve it.

Spiritual Connection: Cartomancy can also provide a spiritual connection for those who seek it. It can offer a sense of comfort, reassurance, and guidance from a higher power or divine presence.

Psychological Healing: Cartomancy can aid in psychological healing by identifying patterns or behaviors that may be holding an individual back. It can also help individuals confront past traumas or emotional blockages and move forward towards healing and growth.

Scope of Cartomancy .

Cartomancy can be pursued as a career by those who have a deep understanding of the art and can provide accurate readings. Cartomancers can work independently by offering their services to clients, or they can work in psychic shops, tarot reading centers, or even online platforms. They can also write books on cartomancy or provide online courses to teach others how to read cards. A career in cartomancy requires a strong connection with intuition, excellent communication skills, and a passion for helping others. Successful cartomancers have the ability to build a loyal client base and create a reputation for themselves as skilled and trustworthy readers.

What are the Tools for Cartomancy ?

The following Tools / Items are needed for Cartomancy :

- Playing Cards Deck
- Wooden Box
- Velvet Table Cloth
- Aroma Candles
- Angel idol

CHAPTER : 2

HISTORY OF CARTOMANCY

- Origin of Cartomancy
- History of Cartomancy
- Vedic History of Cartomancy
- Modern development in Cartomancy
- Time Line of Cartomancy

Practical Manual of Cartomancy

Origin of Cartomancy

Cartomancy, the practice of using playing cards for divination, has a long and varied history. The origin of cartomancy is uncertain, but it is believed to have originated in China or India in the 9th century AD. The use of playing cards for divination became popular in Europe during the 18th century, and it spread to America during the 19th century. In the early days of cartomancy, only the wealthy could afford to have their fortunes read using playing cards, as the cards were very expensive. Over time, however, playing cards became more affordable and accessible, and the practice of cartomancy became more widespread. Today, cartomancy is still a popular form of divination, with many people using playing cards to gain insight into their lives and futures.

History of Cartomancy

Cartomancy, the practice of using playing cards for divination, has a long and varied history. The origin of cartomancy is uncertain, but it is believed to have originated in China or India in the 9th century AD. The use of playing cards for divination became popular in Europe during the 18th century, and it spread to America during the 19th century. In the early days of cartomancy, only the wealthy could afford to have their fortunes read using playing cards, as the cards were very expensive. Over time, however, playing cards became more affordable and accessible, and the practice of cartomancy became more widespread. Today, cartomancy is still a popular form of divination, with many people using playing cards to gain insight into their lives and futures.

Vedic History of Cartomancy

There is no direct reference to cartomancy in Vedic history as cartomancy specifically refers to divination using playing cards which originated in Europe in the 14th century. However, Vedic astrology has a long and rich history of divination using various tools such as numerology, palmistry, and tarot cards.

Practical Manual of Cartomancy

In Vedic astrology, the use of divination tools is deeply rooted in the belief that each individual's destiny is predetermined and can be understood through various forms of divination. This includes the use of tarot cards, which have been used in India for centuries and are believed to have originated from the ancient Hindu text, the Mahabharata.

The Mahabharata is one of the two major ancient Sanskrit epics of India, and it includes a section known as the "Gita Press Gorakhpur edition," which describes a system of divination using playing cards known as "Gyan Chaupar." This system of divination is similar to cartomancy in that it uses a deck of cards to provide insight and guidance.

Additionally, in Vedic numerology, each number is associated with a particular planet or deity, and this system can also be used for divination and guidance. Palmistry, which is also practiced in Vedic astrology, involves the interpretation of the lines and markings on the hand to gain insight into an individual's character, personality, and destiny.

Overall, while cartomancy specifically is not part of Vedic history, the use of divination tools and practices to gain insight into an individual's destiny is deeply rooted in Vedic astrology and has been practiced for centuries.

Modern development in Cartomancy

Modern development in Cartomancy refers to the use of technology and new approaches to interpreting card readings. With the advent of digital technology, online tarot card readings and other forms of cartomancy have become more accessible. In addition, there have been efforts to create new decks with unique interpretations and symbolism that can be used in readings.

One of the most significant developments in modern Cartomancy is the integration of psychology and spirituality in interpreting card readings. This approach recognizes that the cards can offer insight into the unconscious mind and provide a pathway for personal growth and development. Some practitioners of Cartomancy now incorporate meditation, visualization, and affirmations into their readings to help clients better understand the messages of the cards and work towards their personal goals.

Another recent development in Cartomancy is the rise of ethical standards and professional organizations. Some practitioners have established codes of conduct and seek certification or membership in organizations that promote responsible and ethical practices. This helps to ensure that clients receive accurate and beneficial readings and that Cartomancy as a field is respected and valued.

Overall, modern Cartomancy is an evolving field that continues to adapt to new technologies and approaches while preserving the rich history and tradition of card reading.

Time Line of Cartomancy

Cartomancy has a long history, and its evolution can be traced back to ancient times. Here's a timeline of some significant events in the history of cartomancy:

Practical Manual of Cartomancy

9th century : Playing cards are invented in China.

14th century : Playing cards are introduced to Europe via the Islamic world.

16th century : Tarot cards are created in Italy and used for gaming.

18th century : French occultist Jean-Baptiste Alliette, also known as Etteilla, publishes the first book on cartomancy.

19th century : Cartomancy becomes increasingly popular in Europe and America, with various systems of interpretation and divination developed.

20th century : Cartomancy continues to be popular, with new decks and systems being created, such as Lenormand cards and Kipper cards.

21st century : Cartomancy remains a popular form of divination, with many online resources and communities dedicated to the practice.

It's important to note that while cartomancy has evolved over time and has been influenced by various cultures and traditions, its exact origins and development are difficult to trace definitively.

CHAPTER : 3

ANATOME OF CARTOMANCY DECK

- Anatomy of Cartomancy Deck
- Type of Suits
- Type of Cards

Practical Manual of Cartomancy

Anatomy of Cartomancy Deck

Playing cards typically have four suits, namely hearts, diamonds, clubs, and spades. Each suit has thirteen cards that are numbered from 2 to 10, and also include face cards, namely the Jack, Queen, and King, as well as an Ace.

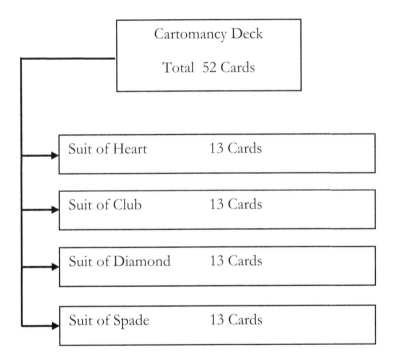

Cartomancy Deck

Total 52 Cards

Suit of Heart   13 Cards

Suit of Club   13 Cards

Suit of Diamond   13 Cards

Suit of Spade   13 Cards

Practical Manual of Cartomancy

Type of Suits

There are 4 Suits in Cartomancy Deck. Each Suits has 13 Cards

1. Suit of Heart   13 Cards
2. Suit of Club   13 Cards
3. Suit of Diamond   13 Cards
4. Suit of Spade   13 Cards

Type of Cards

There are 2 types of Cards in any Suit.

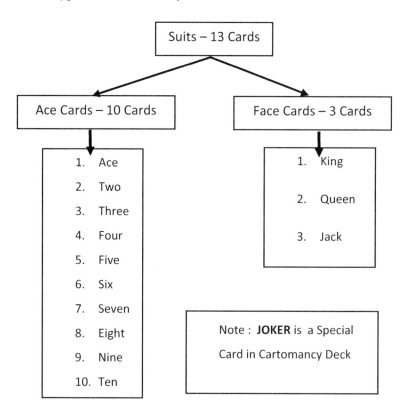

Suits – 13 Cards

Ace Cards – 10 Cards

Face Cards – 3 Cards

1. Ace
2. Two
3. Three
4. Four
5. Five
6. Six
7. Seven
8. Eight
9. Nine
10. Ten

1. King
2. Queen
3. Jack

Note : **JOKER** is a Special Card in Cartomancy Deck

CHAPTER : 4

MEANING OF CARTOMANCY CARDS

- Suit of Heart
- Suit of Club
- Suit of Diamond
- Suit of Spade

Suit of Heart

The heart suit is traditionally represented by a red heart symbol. It represents love, emotions, and matters of the heart. In cartomancy, heart cards can indicate relationships, romance, and emotional well-being.

List of the cards of Suit of Heart

1. Ace of Heart
2. Two of Heart
3. Three of Heart
4. Four of Heart
5. Five of Heart
6. Six of Heart
7. Seven of Heart
8. Eight of Heart
9. Nine of Heart
10. Ten of Heart
11. King of Heart
12. Queen of Heart
13. Jack of Heart

Ace Of Heart

Love: The Ace of Hearts is often associated with romantic love, passion, and affection. It can indicate a new relationship, a deepening of existing feelings, or a strong emotional connection.

Emotional fulfillment: This card can represent emotional satisfaction, fulfillment, and contentment. It can suggest a period of happiness and joy in one's personal life.

Creativity: The Ace of Hearts can also be linked to creativity, imagination, and artistic expression. It may indicate a time of inspiration, creative growth, and the birth of new ideas.

Intuition: This card can be a sign of heightened intuition, sensitivity, and psychic abilities. It may suggest that the seeker should trust their instincts and listen to their inner voice.

Forgiveness: The Ace of Hearts can symbolize forgiveness, compassion, and understanding. It may suggest that the seeker needs to forgive themselves or others in order to move forward.

Healing: This card can be a sign of physical, emotional, or spiritual healing. It may suggest that the seeker needs to focus on self-care, rest, and recovery.

New beginnings: The Ace of Hearts is often associated with new beginnings, fresh starts, and opportunities. It can indicate the start of a new project, a new phase of life, or a new direction.

Abundance: This card can represent abundance, prosperity, and good fortune. It may suggest that the seeker will experience financial or material success, or that they will be blessed with an abundance of love and happiness.

Trust: The Ace of Hearts can symbolize trust, loyalty, and honesty. It may suggest that the seeker needs to trust themselves or others, or that they will be rewarded for their own honesty and integrity.

Divine guidance: This card can be a sign of divine guidance, spiritual protection, and blessings from the universe. It may suggest that the seeker is on the right path and that they are being supported by higher forces.

Two Of Heart

Partnership: The Two of Hearts often represents a partnership or union of two people, whether in a romantic or business context.

Harmony: This card is associated with balance and harmony, indicating that the partnership is likely to be peaceful and mutually beneficial.

New beginnings: The Two of Hearts can also suggest the start of a new relationship or venture that will be important to both parties.

Emotional connection: With its emphasis on the Heart suit, this card highlights the emotional connection between the partners, indicating that feelings are likely to be strong and genuine.

Cooperation: The Two of Hearts is a card of cooperation and teamwork, suggesting that the partners will work together effectively to achieve their goals.

Trust: This card can indicate a high level of trust between the partners, suggesting that they are open and honest with each other.

Support: The Two of Hearts suggests that the partners will be supportive of each other, offering encouragement and assistance when needed.

Intimacy: In a romantic context, this card can represent a growing sense of intimacy and closeness between the partners.

Mutual respect: The Two of Hearts often indicates mutual respect between the partners, suggesting that they value each other's opinions and contributions.

Duality: As the second card in the Heart suit, the Two of Hearts can also symbolize duality, representing the complementary aspects of the partners that make their partnership strong.

Three Of Heart

Love and Affection: The Three of Hearts represents feelings of love, affection, and emotional attachment. It suggests the presence of a loving relationship or a budding romance.

Creativity and Expression: This card signifies creativity, artistic expression, and the ability to express oneself emotionally. It suggests a time of inspiration and artistic pursuits.

Happiness and Joy: The Three of Hearts represents happiness, joy, and contentment. It indicates a time of emotional well-being and satisfaction.

Celebration and Festivities: This card suggests celebrations, festivities, and social gatherings. It is a time for enjoying the company of loved ones and having fun.

Teamwork and Cooperation: The Three of Hearts represents teamwork, cooperation, and harmonious relationships. It suggests that working together with others can lead to success and happiness.

Trust and Support: This card signifies trust, support, and reliability. It indicates that there are people in your life who you can count on for help and support.

Healing and Forgiveness: The Three of Hearts suggests the need for healing and forgiveness in relationships. It signifies the potential for reconciliation and resolution of past conflicts.

Compassion and Empathy: This card represents compassion, empathy, and understanding. It suggests the importance of being kind and compassionate towards oneself and others.

Intuition and Inner Guidance: The Three of Hearts signifies intuition, inner guidance, and trusting one's feelings. It suggests the need to listen to one's inner voice and follow one's heart.

Growth and Expansion: This card indicates growth, expansion, and development. It suggests that positive changes and new opportunities are on the horizon.

Four Of Heart

Love and stability: The Four of Hearts can symbolize a stable and loving relationship, whether romantic or platonic, based on trust, loyalty, and affection.

Family and home: The Four of Hearts can represent the importance of family and home life, and the need for security, comfort, and harmony in one's personal space.

Domestic duties: The Four of Hearts can signify the responsibility and satisfaction of taking care of one's household, including cooking, cleaning, and nurturing.

Stability and balance: The Four of Hearts can suggest the need for stability and balance in one's emotional and mental state, and the ability to handle challenges and setbacks with grace and resilience.

Tradition and values: The Four of Hearts can embody traditional values, customs, and beliefs that bring meaning and purpose to one's life, and the respect for one's cultural heritage and ancestry.

Patience and perseverance: The Four of Hearts can encourage patience and perseverance in pursuing one's goals and dreams, and the faith in one's abilities and talents.

Healing and recovery: The Four of Hearts can indicate the need for healing and recovery from emotional wounds, trauma, or grief, and the support and care of loved ones.

Security and finances: The Four of Hearts can also relate to the material and financial aspects of one's life, such as investments, savings, and property, and the need for security and stability in this area.

Harmony and teamwork: The Four of Hearts can represent the importance of collaboration, cooperation, and harmony in one's personal and professional relationships, and the recognition of the strengths and contributions of others.

Contentment and happiness: The Four of Hearts can express a sense of contentment and happiness with one's life, relationships, and achievements, and the gratitude for the blessings and opportunities one has received.

Five Of Heart

Change: The Five of Hearts represents a change in one's life or situation. This change can be either positive or negative, depending on the surrounding cards.

Instability: This card indicates instability in one's life, with the possibility of unexpected events or emotions that can throw one off balance.

Risk: The Five of Hearts suggests that one may need to take a risk in order to achieve their goals. However, one should be cautious and weigh the pros and cons before taking any risks.

Unrest: This card can signify inner unrest or turmoil. It may indicate a need to address and work through any emotional or mental issues that are causing this unrest.

Loss: The Five of Hearts can also indicate loss, whether it be of a material possession, a relationship, or a personal belief.

Grief: This card may represent grief or heartache, especially if it appears alongside other cards that suggest emotional pain.

Reversal: The Five of Hearts can suggest a reversal of fortune or a change in direction. It may indicate the need to re-evaluate one's choices and make adjustments accordingly.

Inconsistency: This card suggests that things may not be consistent or stable in one's life. It may indicate the need to seek out balance and harmony.

Disappointment: The Five of Hearts may indicate disappointment, whether it be in oneself or in others. It suggests the need to process and move on from this disappointment.

Opportunity: Despite the challenges and instability suggested by this card, the Five of Hearts can also indicate the possibility of new opportunities and growth. It suggests the need to keep an open mind and heart to these possibilities.

Six Of Heart

Harmony in relationships: The Six of Hearts represents a period of harmony and stability in your relationships, whether romantic or platonic. This is a time for peaceful coexistence and mutual understanding.

Emotional balance: This card suggests that you have achieved a healthy balance between your head and your heart. You are able to make decisions based on both logic and intuition, and your emotional life is in a good place.

Home and family: The Six of Hearts can indicate a focus on home and family life. You may be spending more time with your loved ones or making changes to your living situation that bring you greater comfort and security.

Stability and security: This card suggests that you are in a stable and secure position, both financially and emotionally. You may have recently achieved a goal or made progress in an area of your life that brings you greater peace of mind.

Heart-centered pursuits: The Six of Hearts can indicate a time of pursuing activities or goals that are close to your heart. You may be following your passions or exploring your creative side, and finding fulfillment in doing so.

Cooperation and teamwork: This card suggests that you are working well with others and are able to cooperate effectively towards a common goal. You may be part of a successful team or partnership.

Healing and recovery: The Six of Hearts can indicate a period of healing and recovery, either physically or emotionally. You may be feeling better after a period of illness or taking steps to improve your overall health and wellbeing.

Expressing love: This card can indicate a need to express your love and affection to those around you. You may need to make a greater effort to show your feelings or communicate more openly with loved ones.

Romance and attraction: The Six of Hearts can suggest the possibility of a new romance or deepening of an existing relationship. You may be feeling more attracted to someone or experiencing a greater sense of intimacy with your partner.

Generosity and kindness: This card can represent a time of generosity and kindness towards others. You may be feeling more charitable or willing to help others in need, and finding joy in doing so.

Seven Of Heart

Love: The Seven of Hearts is often associated with matters of the heart, and it can represent love and affection. It may indicate a new romantic relationship or a deepening of an existing one.

Good fortune: This card is also known as the "lucky seven," so it can represent good luck and positive outcomes. It may indicate that you will experience unexpected success or good fortune in a particular area of your life.

Happiness: The Seven of Hearts can symbolize happiness and contentment. It may suggest that you will find joy and satisfaction in your personal relationships, work, or hobbies.

Emotional stability: This card can also represent emotional stability and balance. It may suggest that you are able to maintain your composure and handle any challenges or difficulties that come your way.

Spirituality: The Seven of Hearts is sometimes associated with spiritual growth and development. It may indicate that you are on a path of self-discovery and that you are open to new spiritual experiences.

Intuition: This card can also represent intuition and inner wisdom. It may suggest that you should trust your instincts and follow your heart when making decisions.

Trust: The Seven of Hearts can symbolize trust and loyalty. It may indicate that you have strong relationships built on mutual trust and respect.

Inner peace: This card can also represent inner peace and calmness. It may suggest that you have found a sense of tranquility and contentment within yourself.

Creativity: The Seven of Hearts can be associated with creativity and self-expression. It may suggest that you will find inspiration and new ideas that allow you to express yourself in a unique and meaningful way.

Support: This card can also represent support and companionship. It may indicate that you have a strong support system that will help you navigate any challenges or difficulties you may encounter.

Eight Of Heart

Love and romance: the Eight of Hearts is a symbol of emotional fulfillment and happiness in love. If you're single, this card can indicate that you will meet someone special soon. If you're in a relationship, it suggests that your bond

will deepen and become more meaningful.

Commitment: this card can represent making a serious commitment in a relationship, such as getting engaged or married.

Forgiveness: the Eight of Hearts can indicate the need for forgiveness and reconciliation in a relationship or family situation.

Harmony: this card represents harmony and balance in all areas of life, including relationships, career, and personal growth.

Creativity: the Eight of Hearts can symbolize creative inspiration and artistic expression. It may be a good time to pursue a creative hobby or career.

Generosity: this card can represent acts of generosity and kindness, either given or received.

Spiritual growth: the Eight of Hearts can indicate a period of spiritual growth and inner transformation. It may be a time to explore new spiritual practices or beliefs.

Abundance: this card represents abundance and prosperity, particularly in the areas of love and relationships. It may also indicate financial abundance and success.

Healing: the Eight of Hearts can indicate emotional healing and release, particularly from past hurts or traumas. It may be a time to seek therapy or counseling.

Intuition: this card can symbolize the importance of following your intuition and trusting your inner voice. It may be a time to listen to your heart and pursue your passions.

Nine Of Heart

Love and happiness: The Nine of Hearts represents joy and contentment in matters of the heart. It signifies a time of romantic happiness, emotional satisfaction, and the attainment of one's heart's desire.

Commitment: This card suggests a strong commitment to a person or a relationship. It indicates a willingness to make sacrifices for the sake of love and to remain loyal and faithful to one's partner.

Harmony: The Nine of Hearts is a symbol of harmony and balance. It suggests that conflicts and disagreements will be resolved and that the relationship will be characterized by mutual respect, understanding, and cooperation.

Emotional stability: This card indicates emotional stability and a sense of inner peace. It suggests that the querent has worked through past emotional issues and is now able to approach relationships from a place of emotional maturity and stability.

Personal fulfillment: The Nine of Hearts represents personal fulfillment and the achievement of one's goals. It suggests that the querent's emotional needs will be met and that they will experience a sense of wholeness and completeness in their relationships.

Gratitude: This card signifies gratitude and appreciation for the blessings of love and emotional connection. It encourages the querent to express gratitude for the love and support they receive from their partner.

Support: The Nine of Hearts represents emotional support and encouragement. It suggests that the querent's partner will be a source of emotional strength and support during difficult times.

Renewal: This card signifies renewal and rejuvenation in matters of the heart. It suggests that the querent's relationship will experience a new sense of vitality and enthusiasm, and that they will be able to move forward with renewed energy and enthusiasm.

Generosity: The Nine of Hearts represents generosity and kindness in matters of the heart. It suggests that the querent will be generous with their time, attention, and affection towards their partner, and that they will be rewarded with love and affection in return.

Spiritual connection: This card indicates a strong spiritual connection between the querent and their partner. It suggests that their relationship is guided by a higher power and that they are destined to experience a deep and meaningful spiritual connection with each other.

Ten Of Heart

Completion: The Ten of Hearts represents a sense of wholeness and completion in one's life.

Fulfillment: This card suggests that your deepest desires and wishes will be fulfilled in the near future.

Harmony: It indicates harmony in relationships and a sense of emotional fulfillment.

Joy: This card symbolizes happiness, contentment, and joy in all aspects of life.

Abundance: It represents abundance, prosperity, and financial stability.

Success: It signifies success in business or career ventures.

Celebration: The Ten of Hearts often indicates a reason to celebrate, such as a wedding or other significant event.

Satisfaction: It suggests that you are satisfied with your life and your choices.

Gratitude: This card is a reminder to be grateful for the blessings in your life.

Love: It symbolizes a deep, profound love and connection with another person.

King Of Heart

Love and romance: The King of Hearts represents a mature and passionate love relationship, full of deep emotions and commitment.

Emotional intelligence: This card is associated with emotional intelligence, empathy, and sensitivity to the feelings of others.

Trust and loyalty: The King of Hearts suggests trust and loyalty in relationships, as well as the ability to keep secrets and maintain confidentiality.

Fatherly figure: This card may represent a fatherly figure or someone with a nurturing, protective, and supportive role in your life.

Creativity and artistic expression: The King of Hearts can also symbolize creativity, artistic expression, and the ability to channel emotions into artistic endeavors.

Kindness and generosity: This card may indicate a kind and generous person, someone who is willing to give and help others without expecting anything in return.

Spiritual guidance: The King of Hearts can represent spiritual guidance, intuition, and inner wisdom, as well as a connection with higher realms.

Leadership and authority: This card may indicate a leadership role or a position of authority, as well as the ability to make important decisions and take responsibility for them.

Emotional healing: The King of Hearts can also suggest emotional healing, forgiveness, and letting go of past hurt and resentment.

Compassion and understanding: This card may represent someone with a great capacity for compassion and understanding, who is able to offer support and comfort to those in need.

Queen Of Heart

Love and relationships: The Queen of Hearts is often associated with matters of the heart, such as love and relationships.

Emotional intelligence: This card can indicate emotional intelligence, empathy, and compassion.

Nurturing and care: The Queen of Hearts can represent nurturing and caring qualities, such as motherly love and protection.

Intuition: This card may also suggest heightened intuition and psychic abilities.

Creativity: The Queen of Hearts is often linked with creativity and artistic expression.

Domestic life: This card can signify a focus on home and family life.

Femininity: The Queen of Hearts is associated with femininity and the feminine energy.

Kindness and generosity: This card can represent kindness, generosity, and a warm-hearted nature.

Vulnerability: The Queen of Hearts can also indicate vulnerability and sensitivity.

Spiritual growth: This card may suggest a need for spiritual growth and connection with one's inner self.

Jack Of Heart

Youthfulness: The Jack of Hearts is a symbol of youthfulness, energy, and enthusiasm. It represents someone who is full of life and always eager to take on new challenges.

Creativity: This card is associated with creativity, innovation, and new ideas. It suggests that the person is imaginative and has a strong artistic sense.

Emotions: The Jack of Hearts is a card that represents emotions and matters of the heart. It suggests that the person is in touch with their feelings and may be seeking deeper emotional connections.

Relationships: This card is often associated with relationships and romance. It suggests that the person is seeking love and companionship, or may be experiencing a new romantic connection.

Adventure: The Jack of Hearts is a symbol of adventure and excitement. It suggests that the person is open to new experiences and may be embarking on a new journey.

Optimism: This card is associated with optimism and a positive outlook on life. It suggests that the person is hopeful and sees the world as a place full of opportunities.

Playfulness: The Jack of Hearts is a symbol of playfulness and fun. It suggests that the person has a lighthearted approach to life and enjoys having a good time.

Charm: This card is often associated with charm and charisma. It suggests that the person has a natural ability to attract others and may be very persuasive.

Freedom: The Jack of Hearts is a symbol of freedom and independence. It suggests that the person values their freedom and may be seeking to break free from constraints.

Action: This card is associated with action and taking initiative. It suggests that the person is proactive and takes charge of their life.

Suit of Club

The club suit is represented by a black club symbol. It represents work, career, and intellectual pursuits. In cartomancy, club cards can indicate career success, creativity, and intellectual growth.

List of the Cards of Suit of Club

1. Ace of Club
2. Two of Club
3. Three of Club
4. Four of Club
5. Five of Club
6. Six of Club
7. Seven of Club
8. Eight of Club
9. Nine of Club
10. Ten of Club
11. King of Club
12. Queen of Club
13. Jack of Club

Practical Manual of Cartomancy

Ace of Club

Success: The Ace of Clubs often symbolizes success in any endeavor, whether it be in career, relationships, or personal growth.

New beginnings: The Ace of Clubs can signify new beginnings or opportunities in life. It suggests that it is time to start fresh and embark on a new journey.

Creativity: The Ace of Clubs can represent a burst of creative energy, indicating that it is time to explore your artistic or innovative side.

Ambition: This card can represent the drive and ambition necessary to achieve one's goals. It suggests that you should be confident in your abilities and work hard to achieve what you desire.

Intellect: The Ace of Clubs can also represent intellect, suggesting that it is time to tap into your inner wisdom and intellectual prowess.

New love: If you are single, the Ace of Clubs can indicate the start of a new romantic relationship. It suggests that you will meet someone who is intellectually stimulating and who shares your passions.

Financial prosperity: The Ace of Clubs can also indicate financial prosperity and abundance. It suggests that you will experience success in your financial ventures or receive unexpected financial windfalls.

Focus: The Ace of Clubs can represent the need for focus and concentration. It suggests that you need to stay on task and work diligently toward your goals.

Travel: This card can indicate travel or the opportunity to explore new places. It suggests that you should be open to new experiences and travel opportunities.

Mental and spiritual growth: The Ace of Clubs can also represent mental and spiritual growth. It suggests that it is time to expand your knowledge and seek out new spiritual experiences to deepen your understanding of yourself and the world around you.

Two of Club

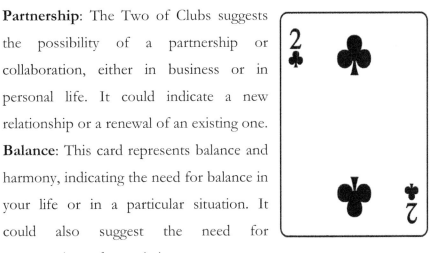

Partnership: The Two of Clubs suggests the possibility of a partnership or collaboration, either in business or in personal life. It could indicate a new relationship or a renewal of an existing one.

Balance: This card represents balance and harmony, indicating the need for balance in your life or in a particular situation. It could also suggest the need for compromise and negotiation.

Decision: The Two of Clubs can signify a decision or a choice that needs to be made. It may suggest the need to weigh the pros and cons carefully before taking action.

Communication: This card represents communication and

exchange, suggesting the need for clear and open communication to resolve any issues. It may indicate the need for a conversation or a discussion with someone.

Planning: The Two of Clubs may indicate the need for planning and organization, suggesting the importance of taking a strategic approach to achieve your goals.

Learning: This card represents learning and education, suggesting the need for self-improvement and personal growth. It may indicate the need to take up a new skill or pursue a new interest.

Conflict: The Two of Clubs can signify conflict or competition, indicating the need to be assertive and stand up for yourself. It may also suggest the need to find a peaceful resolution to any conflicts.

Challenge: This card represents challenges and obstacles, indicating that you may face some difficulties in the near future. However, it also suggests that you have the strength and resilience to overcome them.

Creativity: The Two of Clubs may indicate the need for creativity and self-expression. It may suggest the need to explore your creative side and find new ways to express yourself.

Growth: This card represents growth and progress, indicating that you are on the path to achieving your goals. It may suggest that you are making steady progress towards your objectives, and that you should continue on this path.

Three of Club

Partnership: This card can indicate the formation of a partnership or collaboration that will be beneficial to both parties involved.

Progress: The Three of Clubs is a card of progress and forward movement, suggesting that you are making good progress toward your goals.

Socializing: This card can also represent socializing and spending time with friends or colleagues, suggesting that you will have opportunities for enjoyable gatherings and events.

Creativity: The Three of Clubs is associated with creativity and the arts, indicating that you may have a burst of creative energy or be inspired to start a new project.

Communication: This card can represent communication and the exchange of ideas, suggesting that you may receive important information or have meaningful conversations with others.

Networking: The Three of Clubs is a card of networking and building connections, indicating that you may have opportunities to expand your social or professional network.

Innovation: This card can represent innovation and the introduction of new ideas or concepts, suggesting that you may be able to find creative solutions to problems or come up with new ways of doing things.

Teamwork: The Three of Clubs is also associated with teamwork and cooperation, indicating that you may need to work closely with others to achieve a common goal.

Learning: This card can represent learning and education, suggesting that you may be interested in taking classes or pursuing further education to improve your skills or knowledge.

Planning: Finally, the Three of Clubs can also indicate planning and strategy, suggesting that you may need to carefully consider your options and make a plan before taking action.

Four of Club

Material stability: The Four of Clubs can indicate a stable financial situation and a solid foundation for material success. It suggests that hard work and diligence will pay off in the long run.

Completion of a project: This card can represent the successful completion of a project or venture, and a sense of satisfaction and accomplishment that comes with it.

Consolidation of power: The Four of Clubs can indicate the establishment or consolidation of power, whether it's in a personal or professional context. It suggests that the individual is gaining more influence or control over a situation.

Mental clarity: This card can also represent mental clarity and focus, indicating that the individual is able to think more clearly and make sound decisions.

Practicality: The Four of Clubs can suggest a practical and pragmatic approach to life, emphasizing the importance of practical skills and resourcefulness.

Stability in relationships: In a romantic context, this card can indicate a stable and secure relationship, with a strong foundation of mutual trust and respect.

Home and family: This card can also represent the importance of home and family, and a sense of rootedness and security that comes from having a strong support system.

Loyalty: The Four of Clubs can suggest the importance of loyalty and dependability in relationships, emphasizing the value of trust and reliability.

Order and structure: This card can also represent a need for order and structure, and the importance of establishing routines and systems in one's life.

Conservatism: The Four of Clubs can indicate a conservative or traditional approach to life, emphasizing the importance of established values and beliefs.

Five of Club

Change: The Five of Clubs can indicate a significant change is coming, whether it be a change in job, living situation, or relationship status.

Challenge: This card can also represent a challenge or obstacle that needs to be overcome in order to achieve a goal.

Adventure: The Five of Clubs is a card of adventure and taking risks. It can suggest a desire to try new things and step outside of one's comfort zone.

Competition: This card can indicate a sense of competition or rivalry, whether in the workplace or in personal relationships.

Energy: The Five of Clubs is a card of energy and motivation. It can suggest a need to channel this energy into a productive outlet or activity.

Creativity: This card can also represent creativity and the need to express oneself through artistic or other forms of self-expression.

Travel: The Five of Clubs is sometimes associated with travel, particularly to new and exciting destinations.

Instability: This card can suggest a sense of instability or unpredictability in one's life, whether in relationships, finances, or other areas.

Decision: The Five of Clubs can also indicate the need to make an important decision or choice, and the importance of considering all options before taking action.

Progress: Finally, the Five of Clubs can represent progress and growth, particularly in areas such as personal development and self-improvement. It can suggest a need to focus on one's goals and move forward with determination and confidence.

Six of Club

Success and progress: The Six of Clubs is a card of accomplishment and progress. It indicates that you are making good progress towards your goals and that success is within reach.

Partnership and teamwork: This card can also represent collaboration and teamwork. It suggests that working with others will bring greater success than working alone.

Financial stability: The Six of Clubs can also be associated with financial stability and security. It suggests that you are on solid ground financially and can expect continued stability in the future.

Creativity and innovation: This card can also indicate a period of creative inspiration and innovation. You may be coming up with new ideas or finding creative solutions to problems.

Travel and adventure: The Six of Clubs can also represent travel and adventure. It suggests that you may be embarking on a journey or exploring new places and experiences.

Learning and education: This card can also indicate a period of learning and education. It suggests that you may be studying or acquiring new knowledge and skills.

Social events and gatherings: The Six of Clubs can also represent social events and gatherings. It suggests that you may be attending parties, gatherings or other social events.

Flexibility and adaptability: This card can also represent flexibility and adaptability. It suggests that you are able to adjust to new situations and adapt to changing circumstances.

Growth and development: The Six of Clubs can also indicate personal growth and development. It suggests that you are expanding your horizons and evolving as a person.

Harmony and balance: This card can also represent harmony and balance. It suggests that you are finding balance in your life and experiencing a sense of inner peace and harmony.

Seven of Club

Success in business: The Seven of Clubs often represents good luck and success in business ventures. It suggests that the querent's hard work and perseverance will pay off in the form of financial gains.

Opportunities for growth: This card can also indicate opportunities for growth and expansion, whether it's through education, travel, or new experiences. The querent is encouraged to take advantage of these opportunities to learn and grow.

Inner wisdom: The Seven of Clubs is associated with inner wisdom and intuition. The querent may be guided by their instincts and inner voice, and should trust themselves to make the right decisions.

Negotiations and contracts: In a reading related to negotiations or contracts, the Seven of Clubs suggests that a mutually beneficial agreement can be reached. The querent should approach the situation with an open mind and be willing to compromise.

Mental clarity: This card can indicate mental clarity and the ability to see things clearly. The querent may have a sudden insight or breakthrough that allows them to see a situation from a new perspective.

Collaboration and teamwork: The Seven of Clubs can indicate the need for collaboration and teamwork. The querent may be able to achieve more by working with others towards a common goal.

Communication: This card can also represent effective communication and the ability to express oneself clearly. The querent may need to communicate their ideas or feelings to others in order to move forward.

Planning and organization: The Seven of Clubs can indicate the need for planning and organization. The querent may need to create a plan of action in order to achieve their goals.

Analysis and evaluation: This card can suggest the need for analysis and evaluation. The querent may need to take a step back and assess a situation objectively in order to make an informed decision.

Spiritual growth: Finally, the Seven of Clubs can indicate spiritual growth and development. The querent may be going through a period of self-discovery and seeking a deeper understanding of themselves and the world around them.

Eight of Club

Progress and Advancement: The Eight of Clubs represents progress and advancement in your endeavors. You may have worked hard to get to this point, but now you are finally seeing the fruits of your labor.

Power and Influence: This card can indicate that you have a lot of power and influence in a particular situation. You may be seen as a leader or an authority figure, and people look to you for guidance.

Financial Stability: The Eight of Clubs can be a positive sign for financial stability and security. You may have recently come into money or have a steady income that allows you to feel financially secure.

Discipline and Dedication: This card can represent discipline and dedication in your work or personal life. You may have a strong sense of purpose and are willing to put in the effort needed to achieve your goals.

Organization and Planning: The Eight of Clubs can indicate the need for organization and planning. You may need to make a plan or strategy to achieve your goals and stay on track.

Intellectual Pursuits: This card can represent intellectual pursuits and a love of learning. You may be interested in deepening your knowledge in a particular area or pursuing further education.

Analytical Thinking: The Eight of Clubs can indicate a need for analytical thinking and problem-solving. You may need to approach a situation logically and methodically to find a solution.

Competition and Challenges: This card can indicate competition and challenges that you may face in your endeavors. You may need to be strategic and resourceful to come out on top.

Networking and Connections: The Eight of Clubs can represent networking and making connections with others. You may need to reach out to others for help or support, or you may benefit from collaborating with others.

Balancing Work and Life: This card can indicate the need for balance between your work and personal life. You may need to make adjustments to ensure that you are giving adequate attention to both areas.

Nine of Club

Success: The Nine of Clubs is associated with success, especially in matters related to career or finance. This card suggests that you are on the right track and that your hard work is paying off.

Ambition: The Nine of Clubs represents ambition and drive. It suggests that you have a strong desire to achieve your goals and are willing to work hard to make them a reality.

Innovation: This card is often associated with innovation and creativity. It suggests that you are a forward-thinking person who is not afraid to take risks and try new things.

Entrepreneurship: The Nine of Clubs can also represent entrepreneurship and business ventures. It suggests that you have the skills and mindset needed to succeed in business.

Travel: In some interpretations, the Nine of Clubs is associated with travel and adventure. It suggests that you may be embarking on a journey or seeking new experiences.

Opportunity: This card can also represent opportunities that are available to you. It suggests that you should be open to new possibilities and take advantage of any chances that come your way.

Decisions: The Nine of Clubs can also indicate that you are facing an important decision. It suggests that you should take the time to carefully consider your options before making a choice.

Wisdom: This card is associated with wisdom and learning. It suggests that you are a knowledgeable person who values education and intellectual pursuits.

Change: The Nine of Clubs can also represent change and transformation. It suggests that you may be undergoing a significant transformation or that a change is on the horizon.

Collaboration: Finally, this card can represent collaboration and teamwork. It suggests that you should work with others to achieve your goals and that you will benefit from the input and support of others.

Ten of Club

Completion: The Ten of Clubs represents the completion of a cycle, project or phase in life. It can signify that a goal has been achieved and it's time to celebrate the achievement.

Success: The Ten of Clubs is associated with success and indicates that your hard work and efforts have paid off. It suggests that you have achieved a level of success in a particular area of life.

Advancement: This card can also indicate career advancement or promotion. It may suggest that you are on the path to achieving greater recognition or status in your profession.

Growth: The Ten of Clubs can symbolize personal growth and self-improvement. It may suggest that you have learned important lessons and have grown in wisdom and maturity.

Financial prosperity: This card can be a positive sign for financial matters. It may suggest that your financial situation is improving or that you will experience a windfall of some kind.

Stability: The Ten of Clubs represents stability and security. It can suggest that you have a strong foundation in life and that you are able to weather any challenges that come your way.

Harmony: This card is associated with harmony and balance. It may suggest that you are in a good place emotionally, mentally, and spiritually and that you are able to maintain a sense of inner peace and harmony.

Fulfillment: The Ten of Clubs can indicate a sense of fulfillment and satisfaction in life. It suggests that you are content with where you are and that you are living a life that is true to your values and beliefs.

Wisdom: This card can also represent wisdom and understanding. It may suggest that you have gained valuable insights through your experiences and that you are able to make wise decisions as a result.

Legacy: The Ten of Clubs can symbolize leaving a legacy or making a lasting impact. It may suggest that you are contributing to society in a positive way and that your work will have a lasting impact on future.

King of Club

Authority: The King of Clubs represents a figure of authority, someone who is in charge and has power and control over others.

Leadership: This card can also signify leadership, as the King of Clubs is often seen as a natural leader who inspires others to follow.

Intelligence: The King of Clubs is associated with intelligence and mental sharpness. It can indicate a need to use your intelligence to solve problems or make decisions.

Ambition: This card can also represent ambition and a strong desire to succeed. It suggests that you are determined to achieve your goals and are willing to work hard to make them happen.

Business: The King of Clubs can be interpreted as representing the world of business and commerce. It may indicate that you are focused on your career or a business venture, or that you need to be more strategic in your approach to work.

Strategy: This card can also suggest the need to be strategic and think ahead. It may be a reminder to plan and prepare for the future rather than simply reacting to events as they happen.

Creativity: The King of Clubs can be associated with creativity and innovation. It may suggest that you need to tap into your creativity to solve a problem or come up with new ideas.

Assertiveness: This card can also signify assertiveness and the need to take charge of a situation. It may suggest that you need to be more confident and assertive in your dealings with others.

Mastery: The King of Clubs represents mastery and the attainment of knowledge or skill. It may indicate that you are at a point in your life where you have achieved a high level of mastery in a particular area.

Responsibility: Finally, the King of Clubs can represent responsibility and the need to take on more responsibility in your life. It may indicate that you need to step up and take charge of a situation or be more responsible in your actions and decisions.

Queen of Club

Ambitious and driven: The Queen of Clubs is a natural leader and highly motivated to achieve her goals. She is not afraid of hard work and is willing to do whatever it takes to succeed.

Creative and intuitive: This card represents creativity and intuition. The Queen of Clubs has a knack for coming up with new ideas and finding innovative solutions to problems.

Independent and self-sufficient: The Queen of Clubs values her independence and is not afraid to go it alone. She is self-sufficient and self-reliant, and can handle anything that comes her way.

Strong and confident: The Queen of Clubs exudes strength and confidence. She knows what she wants and is not afraid to go after it, no matter what obstacles stand in her way.

Perceptive and insightful: This card is associated with keen insight and intuition. The Queen of Clubs has a deep understanding of people and situations, and can often see things that others miss.

Charismatic and influential: The Queen of Clubs has a magnetic personality and can be quite influential. She has a way of inspiring and motivating others, and is often the center of attention.

Ambivalent or conflicted: In some cases, the Queen of Clubs can represent ambivalence or conflict. She may struggle to make decisions or be torn between competing interests.

Resourceful and adaptable: The Queen of Clubs is highly adaptable and resourceful. She can think on her feet and find creative solutions to problems, even in difficult situations.

Charming and sociable: The Queen of Clubs is a natural charmer and is often the life of the party. She is outgoing and sociable, and has a way of making others feel at ease.

Impulsive and restless: This card can also represent impulsiveness and restlessness. The Queen of Clubs may be prone to acting on impulse or making impulsive decisions, and may have a hard time sitting still.

Jack of Club

Change and movement: The Jack of Clubs can represent a need for change or the beginning of a new journey.

Communication: This card may indicate the need for better communication in a situation, or the appearance of a helpful messenger or mediator.

Curiosity: The Jack of Clubs can represent an inquisitive mind and a desire to learn and explore new things.

Creativity: This card may suggest the presence of creative energy or the need to tap into one's own creativity in order to solve a problem.

Youthfulness: The Jack of Clubs can be a symbol of youth and vitality, suggesting a time of youthful energy and enthusiasm.

Restlessness: This card may suggest a sense of restlessness or a desire to move on from a current situation or circumstance.

Entrepreneurship: The Jack of Clubs can represent the entrepreneurial spirit, indicating a need to take risks and pursue one's own ideas and goals.

Confidence: This card may suggest a sense of self-assurance and confidence, indicating the ability to take charge and make bold decisions.

Independence: The Jack of Clubs can be a symbol of independence and self-reliance, indicating a need to rely on oneself and take control of one's own destiny.

Leadership: This card may suggest the presence of strong leadership qualities or the need to step up and take charge in a situation.

Suit of Diamond

Diamonds: The diamond suit is represented by a red diamond symbol. It represents material possessions, money, and financial matters. In cartomancy, diamond cards can indicate financial success, investments, and material wealth.

List of the Cards of Suit of Diamond

1.   Ace of Diamond
2.   Two of Diamond
3.   Three of Diamond
4.   Four of Diamond
5.   Five of Diamond
6.   Six of Diamond
7.   Seven of Diamond
8.   Eight of Diamond
9.   Nine of Diamond
10. Ten of Diamond
11. King of Diamond
12. Queen of Diamond
13. Jack of Diamond

Practical Manual of Cartomancy

Ace of Diamond

New opportunities: The Ace of Diamonds can indicate the start of a new venture or opportunity in your life that has the potential to bring you great success and financial prosperity.

Material wealth: This card represents material abundance and financial success. It could indicate a windfall or financial gain, such as a bonus or inheritance.

Positive change: This card can symbolize a positive shift in your life, such as a change in job, a move to a new home, or a new romantic relationship.

Ambition and drive: The Ace of Diamonds can indicate a strong drive to succeed and achieve your goals. This card encourages you to be focused and determined in your pursuit of success.

Entrepreneurship: This card can signify the start of a new business venture or entrepreneurial pursuit, with the potential for great success and financial reward.

Creativity and innovation: The Ace of Diamonds can also represent creativity and innovation, suggesting that you have a unique and original idea that has the potential to bring you great success and prosperity.

Manifestation: This card represents the power of positive thinking and manifestation. It encourages you to focus your thoughts and energy on your goals and desires, knowing that you have the power to create your own reality.

Self-confidence: The Ace of Diamonds can symbolize a strong sense of self-confidence and self-worth, encouraging you to believe in yourself and your abilities.

Courage: This card can also represent courage and bravery in the face of challenges and obstacles. It encourages you to face your fears and take bold action towards your goals.

Gratitude: Finally, the Ace of Diamonds can represent gratitude and appreciation for the abundance and prosperity in your life. It encourages you to focus on the positive aspects of your life and to express gratitude for all that you have.

Two of Diamond

Financial partnership: The Two of Diamonds can indicate a business partnership or financial collaboration that is in the works or being considered.

New opportunity: This card can represent a new opportunity or idea related to career, finance, or material possessions.

Decision-making: The Two of Diamonds can suggest a decision that needs to be made about money, investment, or a business opportunity.

Balance: This card can indicate the need for balance and harmony in financial or business affairs. It may suggest a need to balance work and personal life, or balance spending and saving.

Property matters: The Two of Diamonds can be related to property matters such as buying or selling a home, investing in real estate, or renovating a property.

Communication: This card can suggest the need for clear and effective communication in business or financial matters. It may also represent a message or news related to finances.

Planning: The Two of Diamonds can indicate the need for planning and organization in financial or business affairs.

Positive financial news: This card can represent positive financial news or a small gain, such as a bonus, raise, or unexpected gift.

Doubt: The Two of Diamonds can suggest doubt or uncertainty about a financial or business decision. It may be a warning to proceed with caution.

Flexibility: This card can represent the need for flexibility and adaptability in financial or business matters. It may suggest the need to be open to change or to consider different options.

Three of Diamond

Financial growth: The Three of Diamonds is often associated with financial growth and prosperity. It can indicate that a windfall or unexpected financial gain is coming your way.

Hard work paying off: This card can also indicate that your hard work and efforts will soon pay off, whether it's in your career, relationships, or personal growth.

Collaboration: The Three of Diamonds can suggest the need for collaboration or teamwork to achieve your goals. It may be time to reach out to others and seek their assistance or input.

Creativity and ideas: This card can also represent new creative ideas or opportunities that are coming your way. It's important to stay open-minded and receptive to these possibilities.

Socializing: The Three of Diamonds can indicate a time of socializing and networking. You may find yourself meeting new people or making new connections that can benefit you in the long run.

Travel: This card can also suggest travel or a change of scenery. You may be planning a trip or embarking on a new adventure that will broaden your horizons.

Planning and organization: The Three of Diamonds can indicate the need for planning and organization in order to achieve your goals. It may be time to create a clear plan and take action to turn your ideas into reality.

Taking risks: This card can also suggest taking risks and stepping out of your comfort zone. It may be time to push yourself to try something new or take a chance on an opportunity that presents itself.

Overcoming obstacles: The Three of Diamonds can indicate that you will soon overcome obstacles or challenges that have been holding you back. This can be a time of growth and personal development.

Embracing change: Finally, the Three of Diamonds can suggest the need to embrace change and be open to new experiences. Change can be scary, but it can also bring about positive transformation and growth in your life.

Four of Diamond

Financial stability: The Four of Diamond is often associated with financial stability, indicating that your financial situation is secure and stable.

Hard work and diligence: This card suggests that your hard work and diligence will pay off in the long run, and that you will reap the rewards of your efforts.

Practicality: The Four of Diamond encourages practicality and a down-to-earth approach to problem-solving. You may need to focus on the practical aspects of a situation to find a solution.

Groundedness: This card can indicate that you are feeling grounded and rooted in your life, which can provide a sense of security and stability.

Material possessions: The Four of Diamond can represent material possessions and a desire for material comfort and security.

Solid foundation: This card can indicate that you have built a solid foundation for your life, whether in your relationships, career, or personal growth.

Investments: The Four of Diamond can suggest that it is a good time to invest in something, such as property or a business venture.

Routine and discipline: This card can represent the need for routine and discipline in your life, suggesting that a structured approach will help you achieve your goals.

Value and worth: The Four of Diamond can indicate a focus on value and worth, both in terms of material possessions and personal values.

Conservatism: This card can suggest a conservative approach to life, indicating a preference for stability and caution over risk-taking and adventure.

Five of Diamond

Financial success: The Five of Diamonds often represents financial success and stability. It can indicate a time of prosperity and abundance in terms of material possessions and finances.

Business opportunities: This card can also indicate new business opportunities and ventures. It may be a good time to take a calculated risk and invest in something that has the potential for growth and profit.

Growth and expansion: The Five of Diamonds can represent growth and expansion, both personally and professionally. It may be time to take on new challenges and pursue your goals with renewed energy and enthusiasm.

Materialism: This card can also indicate a tendency towards materialism and a focus on material possessions. It is important to remember that true happiness and fulfillment come from within, rather than from external sources.

Inheritance: The Five of Diamonds can represent inheritance, both in terms of material possessions and personal traits or qualities passed down through generations.

Greed: On a negative note, this card can also indicate greed and a desire for more than what is necessary or reasonable. It is important to maintain a balance between material success and spiritual well-being.

Financial stress: The Five of Diamonds can also represent financial stress and instability. It may be a time to reevaluate your finances and make necessary changes to create a more stable financial future.

New opportunities: This card can also indicate new opportunities for personal growth and self-discovery. It may be a time to explore new interests and pursue new experiences.

Hard work and effort: The Five of Diamonds can represent the rewards that come from hard work and effort. It is important to stay focused and dedicated to your goals in order to achieve success.

Material possessions: Finally, this card can also represent the importance of material possessions in our lives. It may be a time to appreciate the things we have and to cultivate gratitude for the blessings in our lives.

Six of Diamond

Financial improvement: The Six of Diamond is often associated with material success and financial stability. It suggests that the querent's finances are improving or that they are on the right track towards achieving their financial goals.

Business opportunities: This card can also indicate new business opportunities or partnerships that could be beneficial for the querent. It's a good time to invest in new ventures or projects.

Support from family and friends: The Six of Diamond can represent support from loved ones, particularly family and close friends. The querent may feel a strong sense of community and belonging.

Creativity and self-expression: This card is often linked to creativity and self-expression. The querent may be feeling inspired to pursue a creative project or hobby, or they may be expressing themselves more openly in their personal or professional life.

Romance and relationships: The Six of Diamond can suggest positive developments in romantic relationships. The querent may be experiencing a deeper connection with their partner or may meet someone new who is a good match for them.

Stability and security: This card can indicate a period of stability and security in the querent's life. They may feel grounded and secure in their home, job, or relationships.

Material possessions: The Six of Diamond can represent material possessions and physical comfort. The querent may be acquiring new possessions or enjoying the ones they already have.

Generosity and charity: This card can suggest a desire to give back to others and engage in acts of generosity and charity. The querent may be feeling grateful for their own blessings and want to share that with others.

Inner harmony: The Six of Diamond can represent inner harmony and balance. The querent may be feeling peaceful and content with their life and themselves.

Patience and perseverance: This card can also indicate a need for patience and perseverance. The querent may need to keep working towards their goals and be persistent in order to achieve success.

Seven of Diamond

Financial gains: This card often represents money coming in or a positive financial situation. It could signify a pay raise, a successful business venture, or an unexpected windfall.

Material success: The Seven of Diamonds can also symbolize material success and a luxurious lifestyle. It could indicate the acquisition of material possessions or the achievement of a long-term goal.

Opportunities for growth: This card may indicate opportunities for growth and expansion, whether in your personal or professional life. It suggests that you may be presented with a chance to take on new challenges and reach new heights.

Risk-taking: The Seven of Diamonds could represent a need to take calculated risks. It suggests that you should weigh the potential rewards against the potential risks and make a decision based on your analysis.

Inner strength: This card can also symbolize inner strength and resilience. It may suggest that you have the ability to overcome challenges and obstacles and emerge stronger on the other side.

Self-worth: The Seven of Diamonds can also represent self-worth and the recognition of your own value. It may indicate that you are beginning to appreciate your own strengths and talents and are ready to assert yourself in a new way.

Resourcefulness: This card can suggest that you are resourceful and adaptable, able to make the most of the resources you have available to you. It may also indicate a need to be resourceful and creative in finding solutions to problems.

Hard work: The Seven of Diamonds can represent the rewards of hard work and perseverance. It suggests that if you put in the effort, you will achieve success and be rewarded for your hard work.

Harmony: This card may indicate a need for harmony and balance in your life. It could suggest that you need to find a way to balance your work and personal life or that you need to find a way to reconcile conflicting goals or desires.

Generosity: The Seven of Diamonds can also represent generosity and giving. It suggests that you may be in a position to give back to others or to share your resources with those who need it. It may also indicate a need to be more generous in your interactions with others.

Eight of Diamond

Financial stability: The Eight of Diamonds is often associated with financial stability and success. It suggests that you are on the right track and your hard work will soon pay off.

Materialism: This card can also signify materialistic tendencies and a focus on wealth and possessions. Be mindful not to prioritize material goods over more important things in life.

Achievement: The Eight of Diamonds represents achievement and accomplishment. It indicates that you have put in the effort to reach your goals and you will soon reap the rewards.

Career advancement: If you are seeking career advancement, the Eight of Diamonds is a positive sign that your hard work and dedication will be recognized.

Discipline: This card can also represent the need for discipline and structure in your life. It suggests that you need to be more focused and organized to achieve your goals.

Investments: The Eight of Diamonds can indicate good opportunities for investment and financial growth. Be mindful of risks and make informed decisions.

Generosity: This card can also symbolize generosity and sharing wealth with others. It suggests that you are in a position to give back and help those in need.

Stability: The Eight of Diamonds can signify stability and security in your personal and professional life. It indicates that you have a solid foundation to build upon.

Responsibility: This card can also represent the need for responsibility and accountability. It suggests that you need to take ownership of your actions and make responsible decisions.

Hard work: The Eight of Diamonds can indicate the need for hard work and persistence. It suggests that success will come with effort and dedication, so keep pushing forward.

Nine of Diamond

Wealth: The Nine of Diamond is often associated with financial success and abundance. It may indicate that you are experiencing or will soon experience an increase in your material wealth.

Responsibility: This card can also suggest that you have a lot of responsibilities and obligations, particularly related to your career or financial matters. You may need to take on more work or make important decisions regarding your finances.

Risk-taking: The Nine of Diamond can also indicate a willingness to take risks in order to achieve financial gain. It may suggest that you are considering or should consider making investments or taking other financial risks.

Greed: On the negative side, this card can sometimes indicate greed or materialism. It may be a warning not to become too obsessed with accumulating wealth or possessions at the expense of other important areas of your life.

Anxiety: This card can also suggest anxiety or worry related to financial matters. You may be experiencing financial stress or uncertainty about your financial future.

Inheritance: The Nine of Diamond may also indicate an inheritance or financial windfall. This could be unexpected, or it could be something you have been anticipating for some time.

Generosity: While this card can sometimes indicate greed, it can also suggest generosity and charitable giving. You may be in a position to help others financially, or you may be encouraged to give more of your time or resources to charitable causes.

Gratitude: The Nine of Diamond can also be a reminder to be grateful for the financial blessings you have received. Take time to appreciate the abundance in your life and express gratitude for it.

Success: This card is often seen as a positive omen for financial success and achievement. It may suggest that your hard work and efforts will pay off in the form of increased wealth or financial stability.

Security: Finally, the Nine of Diamond can indicate a sense of financial security and stability. You may feel confident in your financial situation and have a sense of peace about your financial future.

Ten of Diamond

Wealth and prosperity: The Ten of Diamond is often associated with financial success and abundance. It can indicate the culmination of a period of hard work and the attainment of material goals.

Completion and fulfillment: This card suggests that a project or goal is coming to an end and that you are likely to feel a sense of accomplishment and satisfaction.

Luxury and indulgence: The Ten of Diamond can also represent a time of enjoying the finer things in life, such as travel, dining out, and other forms of pampering.

Generosity: With abundance often comes the desire to give back, and the Ten of Diamond can indicate a time of generosity and philanthropy.

Investment: This card can also suggest the need to invest in your future, whether that means putting money into a savings account, starting a business, or pursuing further education.

Security: The Ten of Diamond can symbolize a sense of security and stability, both financially and emotionally.

Legacy: This card may also suggest the importance of leaving a lasting legacy, whether that means creating a charitable foundation or passing down family traditions.

Endings and new beginnings: As the last card in the Diamond suit, the Ten of Diamond can also indicate the need to let go of the past and embrace new opportunities.

Responsibility: With abundance comes responsibility, and the Ten of Diamond may suggest that you need to take ownership of your financial situation and make responsible choices.

Gratitude: Finally, the Ten of Diamond can remind us to be grateful for the blessings in our lives and to share our wealth and abundance with others.

King of Diamond

Authority and power: The King of Diamond symbolizes someone who holds a position of power or authority. It can represent a boss, a manager, a leader, or any figure who has control over others.

Wealth and financial security: This card is often associated with financial success and material wealth. It may indicate a windfall or an opportunity for financial gain.

Business and entrepreneurship: The King of Diamond can also represent an individual who is enterprising, business-minded, and skilled in making deals.

Rationality and logic: This card may suggest an analytical, rational, and logical approach to problem-solving. It can also represent an individual who values reason and critical thinking.

Stability and dependability: The King of Diamond may indicate a person or situation that is stable, reliable, and dependable. It can represent a loyal friend or a trustworthy business partner.

Responsibility and accountability: This card may suggest a need for responsibility and accountability. It can indicate that an individual needs to take charge and be accountable for their actions and decisions.

Mastery and expertise: The King of Diamond can represent an individual who has mastered their craft or field of expertise. It may indicate a person who is skilled, knowledgeable, and experienced in their profession.

Ambition and drive: This card may suggest an individual who is ambitious, driven, and goal-oriented. It can represent a person who is willing to work hard and strive for success.

Leadership and influence: The King of Diamond can also represent an individual who has the ability to lead and influence others. It may indicate a charismatic, persuasive, and inspiring person.

Professionalism and formality: This card may suggest a need for professionalism, formality, and decorum. It can represent an individual who is polished, well-mannered, and conducts themselves with dignity and respect.

Queen of Diamond

Abundance and prosperity: The Queen of Diamonds often represents financial success and material abundance. This could indicate that you will receive a windfall or that your hard work will pay off financially.

Socializing and networking: This card can also represent socializing and networking. It suggests that you may meet new people or be invited to events where you can expand your social circle.

Confidence and self-assurance: The Queen of Diamonds is a powerful and confident figure. Drawing this card may indicate that you should tap into your own sense of confidence and self-assurance to achieve your goals.

Creativity and expression: This card is associated with creative self-expression and artistic endeavors. It may suggest that you should explore your creative side or find new ways to express yourself.

Self-care and pampering: The Queen of Diamonds can also represent luxury and indulgence. It may be time to treat yourself to some self-care or pampering, such as a spa day or a shopping spree.

Professional success: This card can also indicate professional success and recognition. It may suggest that you will receive a promotion or be recognized for your hard work in your career.

Charisma and charm: The Queen of Diamonds is often associated with charisma and charm. It may suggest that you should tap into your own charm and charisma to achieve your goals or win people over.

Generosity and philanthropy: This card can also represent generosity and philanthropy. It may suggest that you should consider giving back to your community or helping others in need.

Inner strength and resilience: The Queen of Diamonds is a strong and resilient figure. Drawing this card may indicate that you have the inner strength and resilience to overcome any challenges you may face.

Love and romance: Finally, the Queen of Diamonds can also represent love and romance. It may suggest that you will meet someone special or that your current relationship will deepen and grow stronger.

Jack of Diamond

Ambition: The Jack of Diamond suggests a strong drive to succeed and reach one's goals.

Hard work: This card can indicate that hard work and effort will be required to achieve success.

Resourcefulness: The Jack of Diamond suggests that the querent has the ability to find creative solutions to problems and make the most of limited resources.

Financial opportunity: This card can indicate a financial opportunity or windfall, such as a raise, promotion, or unexpected inheritance.

Impulsiveness: The Jack of Diamond can suggest a tendency to act on impulse, which may not always be beneficial.

Entrepreneurial spirit: This card can indicate an entrepreneurial spirit and a desire to start one's own business or take on new ventures.

Risk-taking: The Jack of Diamond can suggest a willingness to take risks in pursuit of one's goals, but it's important to balance this with caution and careful planning.

Charisma: This card can indicate a charismatic and persuasive personality, which may be helpful in negotiations and networking.

Youthfulness: As a court card, the Jack of Diamond can represent youthful energy, enthusiasm, and a thirst for adventure.

Self-confidence: This card can suggest a strong sense of self-confidence and belief in one's abilities, which can be both empowering and motivating.

Practical Manual of Cartomancy

Suit of Spade

Spades: The spade suit is represented by a black spade symbol. It represents challenges, loss, and endings. In cartomancy, spade cards can indicate obstacles, grief, and difficult transitions.

List of the Cards of Suit of Spade

1. Ace of Spade
2. Two of Spade
3. Three of Spade
4. Four of Spade
5. Five of Spade
6. Six of Spade
7. Seven of Spade
8. Eight of Spade
9. Nine of Spade
10. Ten of Spade
11. King of Spade
12. Queen of Spade
13. Jack of Spade

Ace of Spade

Power and authority: The Ace of Spades is often considered the most powerful card in the deck, symbolizing strength and authority. It can represent someone who is in charge, or who has a lot of influence over others.

Death and endings: In some contexts, the Ace of Spades is associated with death or the end of a situation. This can be a literal interpretation, or it may symbolize the conclusion of something in a more figurative sense, such as the end of a relationship or a job.

New beginnings: On the other hand, the Ace of Spades can also represent new beginnings. This could be a new job, a new relationship, or a fresh start in general.

Wealth and success: The Ace of Spades can be seen as a symbol of wealth, success, and prosperity. It may indicate that good fortune is on the way, or that a windfall is in store.

Misfortune and bad luck: In some cultures, the Ace of Spades is considered a symbol of bad luck. It may represent misfortune, hardship, or difficult times ahead.

Mystery and secrecy: The Ace of Spades is sometimes associated with mystery and secrecy. It can represent hidden knowledge, occultism, or a need to keep certain information hidden.

Intelligence and strategy: The Ace of Spades is sometimes seen as a symbol of intelligence, strategy, and mental acuity. It may indicate a need to think deeply and carefully about a situation, or to use one's intellect to solve a problem.

Courage and bravery: In some contexts, the Ace of Spades can represent courage and bravery. It may indicate a need to face one's fears or take bold action in the face of adversity.

Rebellion and nonconformity: The Ace of Spades can also represent rebellion and nonconformity. It may suggest a need to break free from tradition or authority, or to assert one's independence in some way.

Excellence and mastery: Finally, the Ace of Spades can be seen as a symbol of excellence and mastery. It may indicate that one has reached a high level of skill or expertise in a particular area, or that one is on the path to achieving great things.

Two of Spade

Choices: The Two of Spades can indicate that the querent has multiple options or paths they could take, and they may be feeling unsure of which direction to go in.

Decision-making: Related to the first interpretation, the Two of Spades can signify a need to make a decision, and the importance of carefully weighing the pros and cons before doing so.

Balance: The two in any suit is often associated with balance and partnership, and the Two of Spades is no exception. This card can suggest the need to find harmony or equilibrium in a particular area of life.

Communication: The suit of Spades is associated with the element of air, and thus with communication. The Two of Spades can indicate a need for clear, honest communication with others.

Negotiation: This card can also suggest that the querent is in a situation that requires negotiation or compromise in order to find a solution that works for everyone involved.

Duality: The Two of Spades can represent the concept of duality, such as two sides of an argument or two different perspectives on a situation. The querent may need to consider multiple viewpoints in order to find the best way forward.

Opposition: In some cases, the Two of Spades can indicate a sense of opposition or conflict. The querent may be facing resistance from others, or may be struggling with inner conflicts.

Partnership: As mentioned, the number two is often associated with partnership and collaboration. The Two of Spades can suggest the need for teamwork or seeking support from others.

Planning: The Two of Spades can also be a card of planning and preparation. The querent may need to carefully plan out their next steps in order to achieve their goals.

Analysis: Finally, the Two of Spades can suggest the need for analysis or careful thought. The querent may need to take a step back and evaluate the situation in order to make the best decision.

Three of Spade

Loss: The Three of Spades can represent a loss, whether it be of money, possessions, or something intangible like a relationship or opportunity.

Separation: This card can indicate a separation from someone or something important in your life. It could be a break-up, a move to a new city, or a change in a relationship.

Betrayal: The Three of Spades can symbolize betrayal, either by someone close to you or by a larger organization or system. It can be a painful reminder that not everyone is trustworthy.

Heartbreak: This card is associated with heartbreak and disappointment, especially in matters of love and romance. It can suggest that your heart may be broken in the near future or that you are currently experiencing heartache.

Confusion: The Three of Spades can indicate confusion or a lack of clarity in a situation. It can be a warning to be careful when making decisions or to take time to gather more information before acting.

Turmoil: This card can represent turmoil or chaos, whether it be internal or external. It can suggest that there may be some upheaval in your life, whether it be a change in circumstances or a period of emotional turbulence.

Regret: The Three of Spades can signify regret or a feeling of sadness or remorse over something that has happened in the past. It can be a reminder that actions have consequences and that sometimes we wish we could turn back time.

Grief: This card is associated with grief and mourning, especially in relation to death or loss. It can indicate a period of mourning or a reminder to take time to grieve and process your emotions.

Loneliness: The Three of Spades can represent loneliness or a feeling of isolation. It can suggest that you may be feeling disconnected from others or that you need to seek out new connections or relationships.

Endings: This card can represent endings, whether it be the end of a job, a relationship, or a chapter in your life. It can be a reminder that all things come to an end and that sometimes we need to let go in order to move forward.

Four of Spade

Hard work and effort: The Four of Spades can represent the need for hard work and perseverance to achieve your goals. It suggests that you may need to put in some extra effort to achieve success.

Practicality and organization: This card can also represent the importance of being practical and organized in your approach to life. You may need to plan ahead and be strategic in your actions to achieve your desired outcomes.

Stability and security: The Four of Spades can indicate stability and security in your life. You may have a strong foundation and feel grounded in your current situation.

Limitations and restrictions: On the other hand, this card can also indicate limitations and restrictions that may be holding you back. You may need to assess what obstacles are in your way and find ways to overcome them.

Discipline and structure: The Four of Spades can also represent the need for discipline and structure. You may need to establish routines and systems to help you stay on track and achieve your goals.

Focus and concentration: This card can also suggest the importance of focus and concentration. You may need to eliminate distractions and stay focused on your priorities to succeed.

Mental exhaustion: The Four of Spades can also indicate mental exhaustion and the need for rest and self-care. You may be pushing yourself too hard and need to take a break to recharge.

Learning and education: This card can represent the importance of learning and education. You may need to seek out new information or skills to achieve your goals.

Analytical thinking: The Four of Spades can also suggest the need for analytical thinking and problem-solving. You may need to assess a situation and use your logical and critical thinking skills to find a solution.

Recovery and healing: Finally, this card can also indicate the need for recovery and healing. You may have been through a difficult time and need to take steps to heal and recover before moving forward.

Five of Spade

Loss: The Five of Spades can represent loss or setbacks, particularly related to money or finances.

Disruption: This card can indicate disruptions in plans or sudden changes that can be difficult to adjust to.

Endings: The Five of Spades can represent the end of a project, relationship,

or other endeavor.

Conflict: This card can be a warning of conflicts or disagreements with others, particularly in the workplace or other professional settings.

Breaking away: The Five of Spades can also represent the need to break away from something or someone that is no longer serving you.

Recklessness: In some cases, this card can indicate recklessness or impulsiveness that could lead to negative consequences.

Change: The Five of Spades can also indicate a need for change or a new direction, particularly in creative or artistic pursuits.

Betrayal: This card can be a warning of betrayal or deceit from someone close to you.

Risk: The Five of Spades can represent taking risks, but with the possibility of significant losses.

Transition: Finally, this card can indicate a transitional period, where major changes are happening or about to happen, and a certain level of uncertainty is present.

Six of Spade

Transition: The Six of Spades can indicate a time of transition or change. You may be moving from one phase of your life to another, or you may be in the midst of a significant transition.

Challenge: This card can also represent a challenge that you will need to overcome. You may be facing obstacles or difficulties, but with perseverance and determination, you can overcome them.

Communication: The Six of Spades can also indicate the need for clear communication. You may need to express yourself more clearly or listen more attentively to others in order to resolve a situation.

Analysis: This card can also represent a need for careful analysis and planning. You may need to think critically about your situation and make thoughtful decisions in order to achieve your goals.

Progress: The Six of Spades can indicate progress and forward movement. You may be making steady progress toward your goals or experiencing positive developments in your life.

Responsibility: This card can also represent a need to take responsibility for your actions and decisions. You may need to own up to mistakes or take charge of a situation in order to move forward.

Learning: The Six of Spades can indicate a time of learning and growth. You may be gaining new knowledge or skills that will help you in the future.

Strategy: This card can also represent the need for strategic thinking. You may need to develop a plan or strategy in order to achieve your goals.

Restlessness: The Six of Spades can also indicate restlessness or a sense of feeling stuck. You may be feeling restless or unfulfilled, but this card can also serve as a reminder to be patient and keep moving forward.

Adaptability: Finally, the Six of Spades can represent the need for adaptability. You may need to be flexible and adaptable in order to navigate changes or challenges that arise.

Seven of Spade

Loss: The Seven of Spades can indicate a loss of some kind, whether it be a material loss, such as money or possessions, or a more emotional loss, such as the end of a relationship or the loss of a loved one.

Theft: This card can also represent theft or deception. It may suggest that someone is stealing from you or that you are being deceived in some way.

Betrayal: The Seven of Spades can be a sign of betrayal or backstabbing. It may indicate that someone you thought you could trust is actually working against you.

Challenge: This card can also indicate a challenge or obstacle that you will need to overcome. You may face difficulties or setbacks, but if you stay focused and persevere, you can emerge stronger.

Analysis: The Seven of Spades can represent analysis, logic, and critical thinking. It may suggest that you need to take a more analytical approach to a situation and carefully weigh your options before making a decision.

Restlessness: This card can also indicate restlessness or a need for change. You may be feeling bored or dissatisfied with your current situation and be eager for something new.

Risk: The Seven of Spades can also represent risk-taking and the need to take a chance. You may need to be willing to take a leap of faith and trust that things will work out in the end.

Insecurity: This card can indicate insecurity or self-doubt. You may be questioning your abilities or feeling uncertain about the future.

Illness: The Seven of Spades can also represent illness or physical challenges. It may suggest that you need to take better care of your health or seek medical attention if you are feeling unwell.

Secret: Finally, the Seven of Spades can reveal secrecy, hidden things, confidential things.

Eight of Spade

Betrayal: The Eight of Spades can represent betrayal, as if someone close to you has turned against you.

Danger: This card can indicate a sense of danger or a warning of potential harm.

Loss: The Eight of Spades can be a sign of loss, whether it's financial, emotional, or something else.

Transition: The card can indicate a time of transition or change, whether it's a physical move, a change of job, or a change in

personal relationships.

Failure: The Eight of Spades can indicate a sense of failure or a lack of success.

Isolation: This card can represent isolation or a feeling of being alone.

Loneliness: The Eight of Spades can also indicate feelings of loneliness or separation from others.

Burden: This card can represent a heavy burden or responsibility that you're struggling to carry.

Challenge: The Eight of Spades can indicate a challenging situation or a difficult obstacle that you must overcome.

Secret: This card can also represent secrets or hidden information that you may need to uncover or reveal.

Nine of Spade

Loss: The Nine of Spades can signify loss, whether it be financial, material, or emotional. It suggests a feeling of disappointment or sorrow over something that has been taken away.

Loneliness: This card can also represent feelings of isolation or loneliness. It may indicate a sense of disconnection from others or a lack of emotional support.

Betrayal: The Nine of Spades can sometimes indicate betrayal or deception. It may suggest that someone close to you is not being truthful or that you are feeling let down by someone you trusted.

Anxiety: This card can also represent anxiety or worry, especially about the future. It may suggest that you are feeling stressed or uncertain about something in your life.

Illness: In some cases, the Nine of Spades can represent illness or health issues. It may indicate a need to take better care of yourself or to seek medical attention.

Endings: This card can also signify the end of a chapter or the completion of a project. It may suggest that it's time to move on from something in your life or that you have achieved a significant milestone.

Difficulty: The Nine of Spades can also indicate difficulty or hardship. It may suggest that you are facing obstacles or challenges that are causing you stress or frustration.

Darkness: This card can represent a sense of darkness or negativity. It may suggest that you are feeling pessimistic or hopeless about something in your life.

Secret: The Nine of Spades can also indicate secrecy or hidden agendas. It may suggest that someone is keeping something from you or that you are not being completely honest with yourself or others.

Transformation: Finally, the Nine of Spades can also represent transformation or change. It may suggest that you are going through a period of personal growth or that you are ready to leave old patterns.

Ten of Spade

Endings: The Ten of Spades can symbolize an ending or completion of some kind. This could be the end of a project, a relationship, or a phase in your life.

Transition: The Ten of Spades can also represent a time of transition or change. This card suggests that you may be moving on to something new or making a significant change in your life.

Loss: In some contexts, the Ten of Spades can represent loss or disappointment. You may have experienced a setback or felt let down by someone or something.

Grief: This card can also be associated with grief or mourning. You may be struggling to come to terms with a loss or a difficult situation in your life.

Release: The Ten of Spades can also symbolize the need to let go of something or someone. This could be a negative thought pattern, a habit, or a person who is no longer serving you.

Transformation: The Ten of Spades can be seen as a card of transformation. This card suggests that you may be going through a metamorphosis, whether on a personal or spiritual level.

Challenge: This card can also represent a challenge or obstacle that you are facing. You may be feeling stuck or overwhelmed by a difficult situation.

Reflection: The Ten of Spades can also suggest the need for reflection and introspection. You may need to take some time to think about your life and make some changes.

Wisdom: This card can also be associated with wisdom and insight. You may have gained valuable knowledge or experience through a difficult situation, which will help you in the future.

Regeneration: Finally, the Ten of Spades can represent regeneration or renewal. This card suggests that you have the ability to overcome challenges and start fresh.

King of Spade

Authority: The King of Spades represents a person of great authority and power, who is in control of their domain.

Intelligence: This card is often associated with intelligence, strategic thinking, and problem-solving abilities.

Ambition: The King of Spades can also signify someone who is ambitious and driven, with a desire to succeed and achieve great things.

Leadership: As a natural leader, the King of Spades inspires others to follow their example and make things happen.

Rationality: The King of Spades is a logical, analytical thinker, who relies on reason and evidence to make decisions.

Mastery: This card can also represent mastery of a particular field or subject, indicating a level of expertise and knowledge that others look up to.

Discipline: The King of Spades has a strong sense of discipline and self-control, which helps them to stay focused and achieve their goals.

Independence: This card can symbolize a person who is self-reliant and independent, with a strong sense of their own identity and purpose.

Challenge: Sometimes the King of Spades can indicate a difficult challenge or obstacle that needs to be overcome, requiring courage and determination.

Loneliness: In some interpretations, the King of Spades can represent a person who is isolated or lonely, due to their intense focus on their work or goals, which can sometimes cause them to neglect their personal relationships.

Queen of Spade

Authority: The Queen of Spades represents a person with authority and power, someone who can make important decisions and lead others.

Intelligence: This card can also signify intelligence and sharpness of mind. It suggests that the person in question is able to think critically and make well-informed decisions.

Ambition: The Queen of Spades can also

represent someone who is ambitious and driven, who is willing to take risks and work hard to achieve their goals.

Independence: This card can also indicate independence and self-sufficiency. The person in question is not reliant on others and is able to take care of themselves.

Mystery: The Queen of Spades is often associated with mystery and secrecy. It suggests that there may be hidden agendas or motives at play.

Perfectionism: This card can also indicate a tendency towards perfectionism. The person in question may be very detail-oriented and focused on getting everything just right.

Emotional detachment: The Queen of Spades can also represent emotional detachment and a lack of empathy. This can be a negative trait, as it may indicate a lack of compassion for others.

Ruthlessness: In some cases, the Queen of Spades can indicate a ruthless or cold-hearted person. This may suggest that the person is willing to do whatever it takes to get what they want, regardless of the consequences.

Intuition: This card can also signify intuition and psychic abilities. The person in question may be highly perceptive and able to pick up on subtle clues and signals.

Transformation: Finally, the Queen of Spades can represent transformation and change. It suggests that the person in question is undergoing a significant transformation or metamorphosis, and may be moving towards a new phase of their life.

Jack of Spade

Ambition: The Jack of Spades is a card of ambition and determination. It can represent the drive to achieve one's goals, and the willingness to do whatever it takes to succeed.

Cunning: The Jack of Spades can also signify cunning and trickery. It may suggest the need to be shrewd and strategic in order to outsmart opponents or navigate difficult situations.

Intelligence: This card is often associated with intelligence and quick thinking. It may suggest the need to use one's intellect and problem-solving skills to overcome challenges.

Independence: The Jack of Spades can also represent independence and self-reliance. It may suggest the need to rely on oneself and not be dependent on others.

Resourcefulness: This card can indicate resourcefulness and adaptability. It may suggest the need to be creative and find innovative solutions to problems.

Risk-taking: The Jack of Spades can also represent risk-taking and boldness. It may suggest the need to take risks and seize opportunities in order to achieve success.

Secretiveness: This card is sometimes associated with secrecy and hidden agendas. It may suggest the need to be cautious and keep one's plans or intentions hidden.

Focus: The Jack of Spades can indicate the need to stay focused and disciplined. It may suggest the need to prioritize one's goals and not be distracted by outside influences.

Mastery: This card can also represent mastery and expertise. It may suggest that the individual has developed a high level of skill or knowledge in a particular area.

Unpredictability: The Jack of Spades can also signify unpredictability and instability. It may suggest that the individual or situation is difficult to control or predict.

CHAPTER : 5

STUDY OF SPREAD

- About Spread
- Some useful Spread
- Create your own Spread

Practical Manual of Cartomancy

About Cartomancy Spread .

Cartomancy spread refers to the way a cartomancer lays out and interprets a deck of playing cards for divinatory purposes. A spread is typically a pre-determined layout of cards that is used to answer a specific question or to gain insight into a particular situation. Different spreads have different numbers of cards and different positional meanings, and the cards are typically interpreted based on their position, their suit, and their numerical value.

Some useful Spread

Here are some common Cartomancy spreads:

1. **Three-card spread**: This is a simple spread where three cards are drawn and interpreted to represent the past, present, and future.

2. **Celtic cross spread**: This is a complex spread consisting of ten cards. It covers different aspects of the querent's life, such as past influences, present situation, and future potential.

3. **Relationship spread**: This spread is used to gain insights into a relationship. It can have different variations, but typically involves drawing cards to represent each person in the relationship, as well as the overall dynamics and potential outcomes.

4. **Career spread**: This spread is used to gain insights into a person's career and professional life. It can involve drawing cards to represent the person's skills, strengths, weaknesses,

and potential opportunities.

5. **Decision-making spread**: This spread is used when the querent is facing a decision and seeks guidance. The cards are drawn to represent the different options and their potential outcomes.

6. **Zodiac spread**: This spread involves drawing cards to represent each astrological sign and their corresponding qualities. It can be used to gain insights into different areas of life, such as relationships, career, and personal growth.

7. **Chakra spread**: This spread is based on the seven chakras and can be used to gain insights into a person's spiritual and emotional wellbeing.

8. **Tree of Life spread**: This spread is based on the Kabbalistic Tree of Life and covers different aspects of the querent's life, such as past experiences, present challenges, and potential growth.

9. **Horseshoe spread**: This spread involves drawing cards in a horseshoe shape and can be used to gain insights into a person's past, present, and future.

10. **Gypsy spread**: This spread is a traditional spread used by Romani people and consists of 21 cards. It can provide insights into different areas of life, such as love, health, and wealth.

Create your own Spread

Creating your own cartomancy spread can be a fun and creative process. Here are some steps to follow:

1. **Determine the purpose**: Decide what you want to use the spread for. Is it for a general reading, a specific situation, or a question you have in mind?

2. **Choose the number of cards**: Decide how many cards you want to use in your spread. Most spreads use between 3 and 10 cards.

3. **Choose the card positions**: Decide on the positions of each card and what they represent. For example, you may have a position for past influences, present influences, future influences, obstacles, opportunities, advice, and outcome.

4. **Write down the spread**: Once you have decided on the positions and meanings, write down your spread on a piece of paper or in a notebook.

5. **Practice**: Test out your new spread on yourself or a friend to see how it works. If you find that it doesn't work well, adjust it accordingly.

6. **Use it in your readings**: Once you have finalized your spread, use it in your readings and see how it works for you.

Remember that creating your own spread is a personal process, so feel free to adjust and modify it as needed to suit your needs and style.

CHAPTER : 6

PRACTICAL CARTOMANCY READING

- Preparation
- Invocation & Card Charging
- Shuffling, Spreading & Reading
- Gratitude

Practical Manual of Cartomancy

Preparation for Cartomancy Reading

- Room Preparation
- Table Preparation
- Self Preparation

Room Preparation

1. Prepare your Reading Room before doing Cartomancy Reading. Here are some suggested steps you can follow :
2. Make your Reading Room Peaceful.
3. Use dim light.
4. Use Aroma Candle.
5. Play calming spiritual music in low sound.
6. Restrict the entry of unnecessary people.
7. Keep your sitting chare facing North.
8. Use some spiritual Banner / Posters in your Reading Room.

Table Preparation

1. Use Velvet Table Cloth to spread Cartomancy Cards.
2. Keep Note Pad and Pen on Table
3. Keep Crystal Angel / God / Goddess Idol
4. Keep Crystal Pyramid
5. Use Aroma Candle with pleasant Sandalwood Scent
6. Keep Cartomancy Deck in a Wooden Box

Practical Manual of Cartomancy

Self Preparation

This is very important to prepare yourself to present for Cartomancy Reading. You may follow the following steps :

1. Take Bathe, Wear Comfortable Spiritual Clothes.
2. Wear Crystal Mala , Bracelet, Pendant etc
3. Charge yourself and protect your Aura
4. Keep yourself happy, hopeful and stress free.
5. Please note – Don't do Cartomancy Reading if you are under any acute emotional pressure.

******

Invocation & Card Charging

This is very important to Invoke Angel and to Charge your Cartomancy Cards before reading. You are suggested to follow the following steps :

1. Sit comfortably.
2. Concentrate your mind
3. Invoke Angel
4. Prayer
5. Feel Blessed
6. Keep Cards in your Left hand, cover with Right hand and keep on your Heart.
7. Touch each cards.

******

Practical Manual of Cartomancy

Shuffling, Spreading & Reading

Please follow the following steps for Cartomancy Reading :

1. Pray to Angel and Ask your Client also to Pray.
2. Ask your Client to frame question properly clearly and repeat 3 times.
3. Understand the questions and choose relevant Spread.
4. Shuffle the Cards Spread on Table
5. Tell your Client to pic the Cards according to Spread.
6. See the card, relate with question, use your intuition and predict.
7. Talk to your Client, Counsel him / her.
8. Suggest Remedy if required.

****

Gratitude

After reading express the attitude of Gratitude to each and every thing and person. Thanks to your Angel. Say three Times :
Thanks , Thanks , Thanks

Then pack up your all Cartomancy Tools.

CHAPTER : 7

REMEDY

In cartomancy, a remedy refers to a suggested action or solution to help address an issue or challenge revealed through a reading. The idea behind a remedy is that while the cards can provide insight and guidance, ultimately it is up to the individual to take action in their life to manifest change. Here are some common remedies in cartomancy:

1.   Meditation or Prayer: If the reading suggests a need for spiritual guidance or connection, meditation or prayer may be recommended.

2.   Journaling: If the reading indicates a need for self-reflection or exploration of emotions, keeping a journal may be suggested.

3.   Self-Care: If the reading reveals a need for self-care or physical well-being, recommendations such as exercise, healthy eating, or getting more rest may be given.

4.   Communication: If the reading shows a need for better communication with others, recommendations to improve communication skills, or to have a difficult conversation with someone may be suggested.

5.   Seeking Professional Help: If the reading shows that the issue at hand may require professional assistance, such as seeking therapy or counseling, this may be recommended.

It's important to note that remedies are not intended to replace professional advice or medical treatment. They are simply suggestions to help the individual address the issues revealed through the reading.

GRATITUDE

As I come to the end of this book, I want to express my deepest gratitude to all those who have supported me along the way.

To my family, friends, and loved ones, thank you for your unwavering love and encouragement. Your belief in me has been my guiding light, and I am so grateful for each and every one of you.

To my editor and publishing team, thank you for your tireless efforts in bringing this book to life. Your dedication and expertise have been invaluable, and I am honored to have had the opportunity to work with you.

To my readers, thank you for joining me on this journey. Your support and enthusiasm for my work mean more to me than words can express, and I am deeply grateful for your time and attention.

I hope that this book has brought you joy, inspiration, and new insights. Thank you for being a part of my world, and for allowing me to be a part of yours.

With heartfelt thanks,

RK Sharma

If you want to learn Cartomancy or If you are looking for Consultations. Please contact me.

RK Sharma

Mobile No.   +91 9990 463 463

Email id – rks.rksharma@gmail.com

www.rksharma.org

Printed in Great Britain
by Amazon

40710487R00069